IT Governance to Drive High Performance

Lessons from Accenture

IT Governance to Drive High Performance

Lessons from Accenture

ROBERT E. KRESS

IT Governance Publishing

IT Governance Publishing
IT Governance Limited
Unit 3, Clive Court
Bartholomew's Walk
Cambridgeshire Business Park
Ely
Cambridgeshire
CB7 4EH
United Kingdom

www.itgovernance.co.uk

First published in the United Kingdom in 2010 by
IT Governance Publishing.

ISBN 978-1-84928-037-2

PREFACE

Information technology (IT) is a cornerstone to high performance, according to Accenture research on high performance business. Technology is so pervasive, so embedded in the DNA of any organization, that IT decisions can literally make or break a company's competitiveness and its ability to achieve strategic goals.

Decisions about IT, therefore, are fundamental to the effectiveness of any organization, whether it relies on a handful of applications and systems or hundreds of them. Yet many organizations, of all sizes, lack a formal IT governance system for ensuring IT decisions, investments, policies and processes support their strategies, objectives and market position.

The cost of this negligence can be very high indeed. No matter how cost-effective or flawless the execution, an IT project that doesn't deliver capabilities to support and drive the organization forward is instead holding it back and potentially jeopardizing its future.

At Accenture, IT governance plays a pivotal role in fueling the company's success. It provides an essential framework for making IT decisions that optimize IT's value, the business' use of IT and its IT spending.

In the following pages, this pocket guide will provide a detailed description of Accenture's IT governance. It will show how effective IT governance links IT strategy and IT decisions to Accenture's business strategy and business priorities. It will lay out the elements of its IT governance policy and detail its governance structure.

Every organization needs to create an IT governance model that fits its needs, goals and operating model. Accenture's best-practices approach can serve as a strong starting point or as a benchmark for other IT governance models.

ABOUT THE AUTHOR

Robert E. Kress is the Executive Director of Business Operations for Accenture's high performance IT organization, which directly supports the business goals of a $22 billion company with more than 175,000 employees in 52 countries. Reporting to Accenture's Chief Information Officer, Bob has overall responsibility for running IT like a business. He provides management for the organization's $700 million global IT operation, including direct management of IT governance, IT strategy, IT planning, IT risk office, supplier and contract management, audit and IT policy, communications, business performance, finance, human resources, deployable resources and organizational development.

Bob has extensive experience in IT planning, technology operations, application development, product management, service planning and program management. Before joining the IT operation, Bob was an Accenture consultant. In that role, he developed and delivered large, complex IT transformation projects and business solutions that maximized return on investment for clients in the healthcare, government, and consumer products sectors.

Bob holds a Bachelor of Science in Physics from Loras College in Dubuque, Iowa and a Master of Business Administration from the University of Iowa.

CONTENTS

INTRODUCTION

In the late 1990s, Andersen Consulting was preparing to spin off from Andersen Worldwide, the holding company for the consulting firm and for its sister company, accounting firm Arthur Andersen. Faced with building its own information technology (IT) organization, Andersen Consulting (now Accenture) quickly realized it was taking on a formidable challenge. At the time, the firm operated in more than 40 countries, and each country, and even some regions within large countries such as the United States, had their own IT organizations, systems and processes.

This arrangement was a legacy of how Andersen Consulting grew, as a decentralized partnership with profit-and-loss responsibility residing in the local offices. It was also a recipe for potential disaster as the company prepared to restructure itself as a global public corporation. The finance function alone was using more than 450 applications, which would have made it complicated indeed to produce the consolidated financial reporting required of public companies.

The pending changes in ownership prompted the firm to develop a global IT strategy. Anchoring the strategy is a robust and responsive IT governance model.

A global leader in designing and implementing IT systems and IT governance models for organizations, Accenture defines IT governance as establishing clear responsibility and accountability for making IT decisions and for IT delivery. It relies on two guiding principles for IT governance: IT decisions are aligned with business strategies and IT spending is directed to support those strategies. This approach improves both corporate and IT effectiveness.

From this foundation, Accenture has built a comprehensive set of policies and procedures for prioritizing and implementing IT investments and managing and measuring IT performance.

IT governance contributes to high performance

Accenture's IT governance has been absolutely fundamental to the company's high performance; this is reflected in its strong growth in profits and revenues. Since going public in 2001, revenues have doubled, reaching $21.6 billion in the fiscal year ending August 31, 2009. Operating profits nearly tripled over the same period to $2.6 billion.

According to Accenture research, high- performance businesses develop a strong performance anatomy that allows them to continually execute better than their competitors. A company's IT capability is a key part of its performance anatomy and enables top performers to uncover and swiftly act on customer and business insights, transform business models and create new products and services. A proactive IT governance model also ensures that business leaders participate in IT decisions so they align with business priorities.

To be effective, then, an IT governance model must perform several important functions:

- focus IT investments on business priorities;
- drive cost-effective IT spending;
- enable all constituent groups to have a voice in major IT decisions;
- provide clarity on IT decision-making responsibility for all aspects of IT.

Predicated on its strong IT governance model, Accenture's IT organization effectively and efficiently supports the company's complex business structure. The management consulting, technology services and business process outsourcing giant is highly matrixed, with five operating groups, 19 industry practices and more than 175,000 employees in 52 countries who serve clients in more than 120 countries.

Figure 1: Accenture's matrixed structure

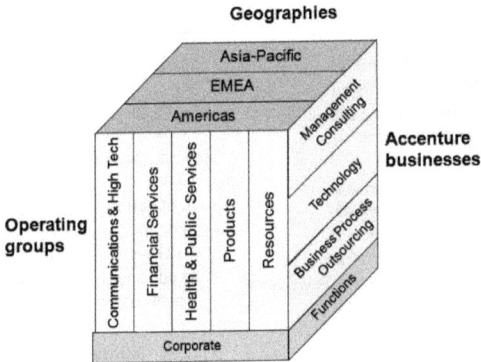

A massive IT operation underpins these businesses and employees, including:

- 150,000+ workstations deployed;
- 6,000+ devices monitored;
- 4,500 servers managed;
- 13,190 megabits/second of network bandwidth managed;
- 356 global applications;
- 195 local applications supported;
- single-instance global SAP enterprise resource planning (ERP) system.

Figure 2: Accenture IT

Hardware and network
- 150,000+ workstations deployed
- 6,045 devices monitored
- 4,538 servers managed
- 13,190 megabytes network bandwidth managed

Websites
- 60,000 unique visitors to the Accenture portal per day
- 30,000 unique visitors to accenture.com per day
- 46,000 unique search queries per day

Applications
- 356 global applications
- 195 local applications supported
- Single instance global SAP ERP

Collaboration
- 177,000 e-mail accounts
- 23,000,000 e-mail messages per day
  - 22,000,000 spam messages blocked
- 2,000 Telepresence hours per month
- 10,448 Sharepoint sites
- 25,000 mobile devices (Blackberry®/Windows®)
- 37,000,000 audio conferencing minutes per month

Support
- 1,016,190 resolved incidents per year through help desk, eSupport, web chat and local support
- 925,890 eSupport logins

Encouraging innovation

IT governance prepares an organization to seize new opportunities. One example is Cloud Computing. Cloud Computing and software as a service represent a new paradigm for how IT is provisioned, used, maintained and upgraded. When is the right time to move to Cloud Computing? Who makes this decision? Are security and data privacy requirements adequately addressed? Well-defined IT governance will address who is responsible for making these decisions and help to ensure the organization is proactively moving forward and taking advantage of new technologies in a cost-effective, secure way.

IT governance also can harness creative solutions from within an organization. At Accenture, employees from time to time would develop technology tools or gadgets to solve a problem they were having or create a shortcut. Before long, they had spread all over the organization. Some caused problems because they did not fit with the firm's technology strategy or environment. Others were underleveraged since there was no formal program to scale and roll them out.

Accenture engaged its IT governance model to channel its employees' enthusiasm and problem- solving skills. The company created an internal website for employees to communicate creative ideas and needs and build simple tools that can make their daily jobs easier. The IT governance process vets the successful tools to ensure they support the firm's IT and business strategy, then the IT organization develops them for company- wide use.

One success from this approach has been an e-mail attachment handler, which allows employees to avoid capacity problems when their mailboxes fill up with PowerPoint® presentations and other big attachments. The tool automatically strips off the attachment and saves it to the employee's hard drive, then inserts a hot link to the file. If the employee forwards the e-mail, the program locates the file in the hard drive and reattaches it.

Reinventing IT

Accenture's IT governance model enabled the company to reinvent its IT operation, transforming it into a true service organization that operates like a business within a business. Running IT like a business rather than adhering to the traditional model of managing IT as a cost-center sharpens the IT organization's focus on serving its internal customers: Accenture's business units and their employees.

Within the IT governance framework, the new operating model puts more IT decisions in its customers' hands. The IT organization moved to a managed services approach that allows its customers to better meet their business needs by choosing from a portfolio of IT products and services with varying service levels and prices. As part of its IT governance framework, Accenture also establishes and tracks key metrics to quantify the business benefits of IT initiatives.

The customer-focused operating model has fundamentally improved Accenture's IT effectiveness and efficiency while significantly lowering IT costs. The company halved IT spending as a percent of net revenues between fiscal years 2001 and 2009. It cut actual IT spending by 24% during the same period, when the number of Accenture employees more than doubled. In addition, employee and business sponsor satisfaction with IT products and services has improved by more than 20%.

Accenture also now can measure IT's contribution to its business. Using its internal audit group to determine benefits achieved versus projected benefits, Accenture found that IT initiatives delivered an average benefit of 124% — considerably higher than estimates from the original investment business cases.

Best practices in IT governance

Given IT's ubiquity and criticality to any operation, a growing number of organizations are developing more systematic and formal approaches to IT decision-making. In a 2008 survey of 9,500 IT leaders, Gartner Group found 67.4% of companies to be implementing or enhancing their IT governance, while 23.2% were considering such an initiative. More than three out of four, or 77% believed effective governance policies to be important or very important.

While many organizations acknowledge IT governance's importance, they do not always understand how to develop and implement an effective approach. Both clients and non-clients alike regularly seek out Accenture for its expertise on IT governance. Just in the past six months, the company met with more than 20 CIOs of Global 2000 companies, as well as IT leaders from large government organizations, to discuss Accenture's IT governance.

State of the art in IT governance changes, just as business does. In the past decade, Accenture has adapted its IT governance to match the company's evolving needs and goals. The company initiated a formal IT governance approach in 1998 with a limited model that set priorities for IT organization-funded initiatives and investments by involving business executives in the decision- making. Building on its initial successes, Accenture has strengthened its IT governance into its current model, which is comprehensive, innovative and flexible.

CHAPTER 1: SETTING AN IT GOVERNANCE POLICY

Before Accenture's IT governance model was fully implemented, nothing drove home its value more vividly than several notable failed IT initiatives. One was a global markets portal that employees did not end up using and had to be written off. In another case, an electronic scheduling application was selected based on an operating group relationship rather than an independent product review. After four years, the costly tool ceased to meet business requirements and had to be replaced.

These missteps led Accenture to expand the scope of its IT governance model. They also reinforced the importance of adhering to its IT strategic plan, which comes to life through the day-to-day application of its governance model.

Starting with IT strategy

Accenture's IT strategic plan is more than a technology strategy. It begins with a business strategy for the IT organization. The IT business strategy enumerates key goals, such as continuing to shift IT spending to Accenture growth areas and supplying easy access to the best knowledge capital in the industry. It then describes its plans for achieving its goals, including such issues as sourcing, locations, and setting and measuring key performance indicators.

The strategic plan also includes a technology strategy that complements the IT business strategy.

The technology strategy outlines the plans for system architecture, data centers, applications, networks and other IT.

In designing an IT governance policy to support its IT strategy, Accenture kept three primary business outcomes in mind:

- clear IT decision-making authority and accountability;
- targeted IT spending: both initiatives and operating expense should be focused on the most critical business

priorities;
- end-to-end service accountability: the IT organization remains responsible for everything related to internal IT, ranging from IT customer relationship management and service planning to service delivery, even if it outsources some of its IT operations.

Governing principles

The overriding principle is keeping the business at the center of IT. So just as the IT strategy supports Accenture's business strategy, the IT governance model follows corporate governance.

Accenture is structured around global business processes, such as personnel scheduling, financial reporting and procurement. So it has a bias toward central, common IT capabilities, which it accomplishes by standardizing software and systems globally.

However, Accenture balances the advantages of standardization with meeting specific business needs that sometimes require specialized software or tools in a specific geographic region. Due to
individual country laws and regulations, for example, Accenture finds it makes more sense to have country-specific software supporting payroll functions.

In setting IT governance policy, one complicating factor is that all of Accenture's businesses routinely develop IT-based offerings for their clients. When a technology is used for running Accenture, the company's IT organization takes the lead. However, if a technology underpins a client offering, then the business unit leader developing the offering spearheads the IT decision-making.

Other governing principles for IT decisions are:

- enable 'all the time, everywhere' IT capabilities that are readily available for a global, mobile workforce;
- support a shared-services approach for internal IT;
- facilitate self-service.

Accountability is key

Importantly, Accenture's policy doesn't just stop with a framework for initial IT decisions. It follows the life cycle of the technology and covers decisions about delivering, managing, refreshing and replacing it.

The full circle also includes assigning accountability for the financial and operational results of IT investments. IT investment and initiative governance, including the link to return on investment, is covered in more detail in Chapters 2, 3 and 4.

CHAPTER 2: BUILDING AN IT GOVERNANCE STRUCTURE

After constructing its IT governance policy, Accenture created a structure for carrying out the policy. To fit the needs of its matrixed organization, Accenture established five central roles in the IT governance process. They are:

- Accenture Capital Committee
- IT Steering Committee (ITSC)
- IT organization
- business sponsor
- stakeholder.

Accenture Capital Committee

Accenture's Capital Committee, made up of the company's senior leadership, approves all capital investments for the firm. In addition, regardless of whether an IT investment is capitalized or expensed, the committee sets the overall IT investment funding level and provides guidance for IT spending across IT investment categories.

In recent years, Accenture has executed a major about-face on how it finances IT investments. After reaching a point where nearly 40% of its annual IT budget was locked into depreciation and capital charges on IT assets, including capitalized projects, the firm shifted to expensing most IT investments. The change gives it greater flexibility to ramp up or down its IT spending.

IT Steering Committee (ITSC)

The ITSC does much of the heavy lifting in the IT governance process. As the central governing body for IT, its goal is to maximize the long-term business value from IT spending. Its executive sponsor is Accenture's Chief Operating Officer.

The ITSC is chaired by the CIO and is composed of the

Chief Operating Officers (COOs) of every business unit, the Chief Technology Officer, and the corporate leaders for finance, human resources, geographic services and strategy. As ITSC members, they are called upon to represent their individual business units and functions, but also, and importantly, to think broadly about Accenture's needs.

Figure 3: IT Steering Committee membership

Operating groups	Accenture businesses	Corporate functions and geographic services
Products, COO	Management Consulting, COO	Growth and Strategy, Managing Director
Health and Public Services, COO		
	Business Process Outsourcing, COO	Finance, COO
Resources, COO		Human Resources, COO
Financial Services, COO	Technology, COO	
Communications and High Tech, COO	CTO	Geographic Services, COO

This approach helps Accenture prioritize funding requests, which always exceed its annual budget and resources. For example, a couple of years ago, Accenture's Chief HR Officer assembled eight IT requests for ITSC consideration. But after listening to other IT funding requests, she decided to pull three of her HR proposals because she felt it was more important for the company to pursue some of the other proposed initiatives that year.

The ITSC's responsibilities include:

- approving the IT strategy, enterprise architecture, IT initiatives, IT product and service plan, fiscal-year priorities, fiscal-year IT initiative plan and fiscal-year IT capital plan;
- confirming the IT sourcing plan;
- reviewing the fiscal-year IT operating plan at a summary level; and
- ensuring actual vs. projected benefits are measured.

The ITSC meets 'in person' using telepresence visual conferencing twice a year for a day or day- and-a-half sessions. They also convene via conference call four to six times a year.

IT organization

Led by Accenture's CIO, the IT organization is responsible for the firm's internal information technology, including strategy, planning and execution. It manages the relationship with its internal customers, Accenture's business units, including developing technology requirements, strategies and service plans to support business requirements.

The IT organization also owns and manages the business relationships with its IT outsourcing providers, which are Accenture business units. Accenture's outsourcing units deliver infrastructure services and applications development and support for the company. Just as with external providers, the IT group manages the 'internal' outsourcing relationships through signed agreements that specify cost and service levels to meet the company's business and technology requirements.

Business sponsors

Business sponsors are senior executives who are responsible for global business capabilities or business processes, such as:

- sales
- marketing
- client service delivery
- human resources
- quality
- finance.

Some business sponsors serve on the IT Steering Committee. In other cases, the business sponsors are executives who are responsible for a sub-process and do not serve on the ITSC.

Business sponsors are responsible for developing a two-to-three-year strategy and capabilities plan for their global capability. They work with the IT organization to develop technology to support and improve their capabilities. Business sponsors also develop IT investment requests to bring before the ITSC for review, and hopefully, approval.

No investment cases go before the ITSC without a business sponsor. While the IT organization can be a business sponsor for IT infrastructure investments, under this arrangement, it would not propose, say, a new treasury management system.

It is up to the Chief Financial Officer, working with IT, to determine if new technology is needed to better manage the treasury function.

Once approved and implemented, business sponsors work to accelerate adoption and effective use of the new IT capabilities. They also are held accountable for realizing the benefits projected in the investment business cases.

Stakeholders

Business sponsors work closely with stakeholders; these are Accenture executives who represent users of key business processes or business capabilities. Stakeholder executives help define business requirements and implement IT-driven improvements to business capabilities.

For example, Accenture's global HR leader is responsible for its business capability to deploy employees for client work. To improve this capability, the HR leader built a case for implementing a new tool to facilitate scheduling employees on consulting and outsourcing engagements. Stakeholders include all of Accenture's businesses and industry practices, so the top executives of those operating units were heavily involved in designing the business requirements and other facets of the new personnel scheduling process and system.

Figure 4: IT governance roles and responsibilities

Definitions
R Responsible
A Accountable
C Consulted
I Informed

	KEY DECISION AREAS	CAPITAL COMMITTEE	COO	ITSC & IT INVESTMENT SUBCOMMITTEES	CIO	SPONSORS*
Strategy and structure	IT strategy (including policy formation, strategic scorecard, etc.)	I	C	A	R	C (their portion)
	Enterprise architecture (including IT standards)	-	C	A	R	C (their portion)
	IT organization	-	A	C	R	-
Multi-year planning	IT initiatives (categories, budgets, major programs)	A	C	C	R	R (their initiatives)
	IT product and service plan (including global / local accountability)	-	C	A	R	C (their portion)
	IT strategic sourcing plan	-	C (exception)	C	A/R	C (their portion)
Annual planning	Fiscal year IT priorities	-	C	C	A/R	I
	IT investment budget target	A	C	C	R	R
	Fiscal year IT initiative plan	C	C	A	R	A (their initiatives)
	Fiscal year IT operating plan	-	A	C	R	C (their portion)
	Fiscal year IT capital plan	-	A	I	R	C (their portion)
Execution	Variances, changes, issues, performance targets and plans	C (> $10M)	C (> $10M)	A (> $1M)	R	C (operating) R (initiative)
	Benefits realization	I	A (overall)	I	R	A (initiative)/R

* Note (*see Figure 4*): Sponsors can be anywhere within the Accenture organization and can sponsor initiatives, applications or infrastructure services.

Top management sets the tone

Getting the right level of leadership involved in the IT governance process is critical to its success. When Accenture's IT organization drafted its IT governance model, it recommended the business unit Chief Operating Officers (COOs) and other corporate leaders play a major role. Accenture's COO signed off on this approach, and it became central to IT governance.

In fact, leadership involvement is such a priority that COOs who cannot attend an IT Steering Committee meeting have two choices: Simply not be represented at that session or delegate up, to their Chief Executive Officers (CEOs). Delegating down is not an option.

Commitment from top leadership is crucial whether an organization is centralized, like Accenture, or a collection of independent subsidiaries. With a subsidiary-level IT governance model, success would hinge on the direct involvement of the business unit's CEO or COO. The top executives can ensure IT strategy and decisions are aligned with the subsidiary's strategy and priorities. They also can provide the necessary support to implement new technology and drive the resulting business change as well as to facilitate buy-in and adoption.

For decentralized organizations, IT governance could follow a combination approach. Decisions regarding the core IT infrastructure, including networks and data centers, could be centralized along with the technology itself. Applications and other business-specific needs could be addressed through IT governance at the subsidiary level.

CHAPTER 3: LEVERAGING THE STRUCTURE

To cover other major IT decisions, Accenture has mapped out additional responsibilities and accountabilities among the same five governance groups:

- managing global vs. local needs;
- integrating governance with planning and budgeting;
- managing benefit realization.

Global vs. local

Like all corporations and not-for-profit organizations with locations scattered across the globe, Accenture sometimes faces a tug-of-war of interests over single global capabilities or multiple capabilities designed to meet specific local needs. In many cases, Accenture's managed services model solves this dilemma.

The company's geographic leaders are responsible for the local infrastructure and local application and support needs of the geographic units, including personal computers, e-mail, Internet connections and remote access, technology support, and so on. Instead of a one-size-fits-all approach, geographic leaders select from a menu of IT products and services to meet their business requirements. For instance, Accenture offers five capacity options for e-mail, with pricing based on e-mail box size.

When it comes to a process or business capability, the business sponsor is responsible for the global vs. local decision and has the final say. The sponsor solicits input from stakeholders about their needs, and then works with the IT organization to see if it can buy and/or customize or design a single product that meets the business requirements.

It often comes down to a judgment call by the business sponsors. If a product can meet 90% of the requirements, for instance, the sponsor must decide if it is worth the business and technology headaches of having multiple products to fulfill 100% of the requirements.

In terms of recruiting, the global HR leader determined that two applications make more sense than one. In consulting with the various Accenture stakeholders, the sponsor found that recruiting for Accenture's global delivery centers in low-cost countries is sufficiently different than for the rest of the firm that the centers need their own system.

In another example, Accenture's business process outsourcing (BPO) units manage their businesses quite differently than the consulting business. The BPO businesses provide common services to many clients while the consulting unit customizes its services to suit each client. To accommodate BPO, the company is reconfiguring its SAP system to provide a product costing capability.

Integrating with planning and budgeting

The IT organization leads an annual IT investment budgeting process that produces an approved IT investment budget for the next fiscal year, sets the budget for each of five IT investment categories, and sets the spending amount for IT projects deemed necessary by top management. At this point, Accenture's IT investment governance process, which is described in Chapter 4, takes over to allocate the budget across specific projects.

Accenture adjusts budgets as necessary over the course of the fiscal year as business needs arise. Business sponsors can bring investment requests to the IT Steering Committee any time during the year if they consider them too urgent to wait for the annual budgeting cycle. The ITSC weighs the business cases and may slow down or defer other projects to accommodate new priorities.

Establishing and measuring target benefits

About four years ago, Accenture expanded its governance to focus on realizing the benefits associated with technology investments, and not just on managing the investment decision itself. It aimed to inject more rigor and discipline into the process, particularly since some business cases had projected substantial benefits that fell short after implementation.

This feature, which is unique to Accenture's governance model, has proven highly effective. Not only has it sharpened the accuracy of business cases, but it has enabled Accenture to quantify the return on its IT investments — a rare feat among major corporations.

Its governance now covers responsibility and accountability for IT initiative delivery and business benefits, with the business sponsor ultimately responsible for all phases. As part of the business case, business sponsors estimate both hard benefits, such as the annual cost savings from reducing the number of employees needed to perform a function because of the new technology, and soft benefits, such as increased employee satisfaction.

Accenture then measures these benefits for three years after implementation. To facilitate the process, Accenture's IT organization developed a tool that business sponsors use to record the actual business benefits. The IT organization then consolidates measurements for all of the individual projects and produces a report for the IT Steering Committee, Accenture's COO, and the Capital Committee.

The sponsors and CIO then meet with Accenture's COO to conduct a review of individual business cases where there are significant variances in benefits realized vs. planned. In addition, Accenture's internal audit group performs annual reviews of a random subset of business cases. The Capital Committee, ITSC and IT initiative subcommittees receive the review's findings of actual results compared to projections. Importantly, the ability of the business sponsor to achieve the proposed benefits is a consideration in funding future IT investments advocated by that business sponsor.

The case for visual conferencing

Several years ago, Accenture's COO and CIO presented a business case to the IT Steering Committee for implementing state of the art visual conferencing. The collaboration technology, called telepresence, uses high-definition video and high-end audio to create virtual meetings.

The business case said the new technology would allow Accenture clients and employees to participate in 'face-to-face' meetings while reducing travel costs and the associated environmental impacts. The business case called for an initial installation cost of $2.5 million and annual operating costs of $7 million for 35 telepresence sites. The case projected savings of $17 million over a two-and-a-half year period.

Accenture's COO and CIO have more than delivered on that business case. Telepresence has been an unmitigated success. Accenture is saving three times the monthly telepresence operating costs through reduced travel. In fiscal year 2009 alone, total savings from reduced travel were $16 million. Given its demonstrable value, the company has expanded the scope, bringing on more than 50 telepresence sites so far. It expects to add another 10-15 sites in the next year.

Figure 5: Telepresence

CHAPTER 4: CASCADING IT GOVERNANCE

Within its governance framework, Accenture has spelled out governance procedures for multiple IT areas, including investments, products and services, standards and architecture.

IT investment governance

After the Capital Committee establishes annual budget targets, the IT Steering Committee oversees the IT investment and initiative decision-making processes. The IT governance process groups investment requests into five categories, based primarily on the beneficiary of the investment:

- individual businesses
- company-wide
- corporate function (such as finance or HR)
- IT function
- legal and regulatory.

Each category has an ITSC subcommittee, made up of ITSC members, that reviews the cases that fall into its domain. Each committee typically evaluates 30 to 50 business cases, then selects the most critical and prioritizes them within the constraints of the budget guidelines set by the Accenture Capital Committee.

The full ITSC reviews the priority projects from each subcommittee and then approves a final set of initiatives. In doing so, it may reallocate some funding among categories as needed. This initiative planning process generates a comprehensive and rationalized set of business cases requested by business sponsors in each investment category.

Once initiatives are approved, Accenture forms a project steering committee for every major initiative. The business sponsor and IT organization determine who sits on each project steering committee, which typically includes major project stakeholders.

Membership varies based on the project's scope and importance. When Accenture converted the company to a single global SAP enterprise resource planning (ERP) platform, for example, the COO, CIO, CFO and other top leaders were members of the project steering committee. A new financial reporting system might involve the CFO, controllers from several countries, executives representing the consulting and outsourcing businesses, and several IT experts.

Once an initiative is approved, all significant changes to scope, budget, schedule or projected benefits require approval from the project steering committee and the ITSC.

Figure 6: IT investment categories

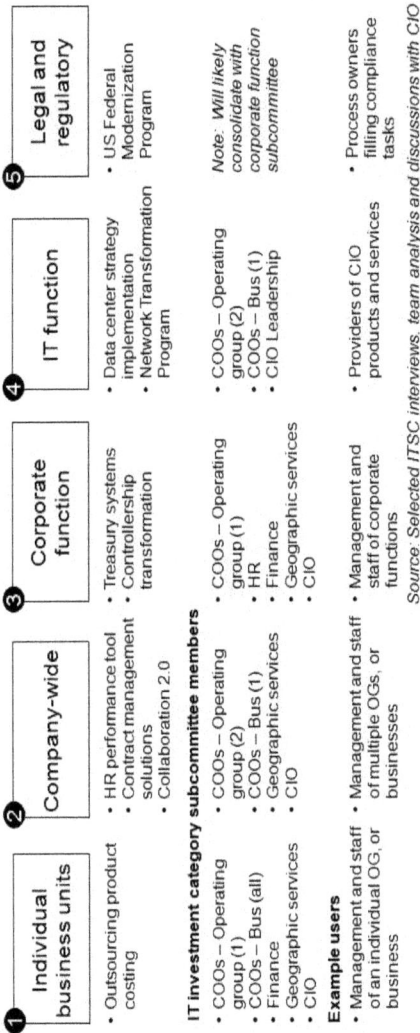

① Individual business units	② Company-wide	③ Corporate function	④ IT function	⑤ Legal and regulatory
• Outsourcing product costing	• HR performance tool • Contract management solutions • Collaboration 2.0	• Treasury systems • Controllership transformation	• Data center strategy implementation • Network Transformation Program	• US Federal Modernization Program

IT investment category subcommittee members

• COOs – Operating group (1) • COOs – Bus (all) • Finance • Geographic services • CIO	• COOs – Operating group (2) • COOs – Bus (1) • Geographic services • CIO	• COOs – Operating group (1) • HR • Finance • Geographic services • CIO	• COOs – Operating group (2) • COOs – Bus (1) • CIO Leadership	*Note: Will likely consolidate with corporate function subcommittee*

Example users

• Management and staff of an individual OG, or business	• Management and staff of multiple OGs, or businesses	• Management and staff of corporate functions	• Providers of CIO products and services	• Process owners filling compliance tasks

Source: Selected ITSC interviews, team analysis and discussions with CIO

IT product and service governance

IT product and service governance clarifies who has responsibility for creating and delivering IT products and services to support Accenture's business operations. It is essentially how the company's IT organization is run.

The IT organization provides the technology infrastructure and the applications to run Accenture's business. Operating units, on the other hand, are responsible for client service IT-based offerings – including deciding where to source the development and delivery of the technology.

In terms of infrastructure, Accenture's IT organization controls all data centers/hosting and wide-area and local-area networks for both data and voice in Accenture-owned facilities. The IT group is responsible for all Accenture-owned personal computers as well as for providing local technology support and help-desk functions.

Similarly, working jointly with businesses, the IT organization makes decisions about applications used to run Accenture, covering everything from company portals and collaboration tools to SAP and integrated forecasting software.

Figure 7: IT governance: five key roles

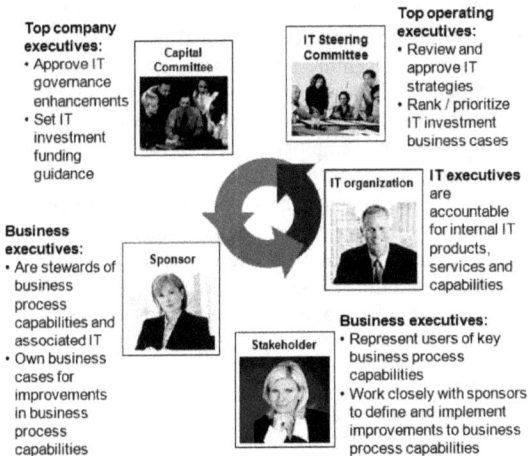

Top company executives:
• Approve IT governance enhancements
• Set IT investment funding guidance

Capital Committee

IT Steering Committee

Top operating executives:
• Review and approve IT strategies
• Rank / prioritize IT investment business cases

IT organization

IT executives are accountable for internal IT products, services and capabilities

Business executives:
• Are stewards of business process capabilities and associated IT
• Own business cases for improvements in business process capabilities

Sponsor

Stakeholder

Business executives:
• Represent users of key business process capabilities
• Work closely with sponsors to define and implement improvements to business process capabilities

Supporting managed services

Like Accenture, a growing number of technology-forward organizations are switching, or already have switched, from the old-school approach of running IT as a set of business applications and costs. Instead, they now offer a catalog of IT products and services.

As in all things IT, a managed services approach depends on strong IT governance. Accenture's IT governance spells out the processes and responsibilities within the IT organization to ensure its managed services fit the needs of the businesses.

The company's IT organization has assigned account representatives to work with each of its 13 geographic regions. The account representatives consult with their geographic leaders and regional business executives to understand their technology requirements. In addition, all products and services, from e-mail to visual conferencing, have a product manager. The product managers get a steady stream of input from the account representatives to help with developing their product strategies, including when to introduce new technologies and when to replace existing ones.

While many of its employees' personal technology needs are common across Accenture's businesses, sometimes a business unit can benefit from a customized product or service. An example is an offering called e-mail forwarding, which is frequently used by employees of Accenture's outsourcing business units. Many outsourcing clients provide e-mail boxes for their Accenture client teams, so the Accenture employees can opt to have their company e-mail automatically forwarded to the client-provided e-mail address. The offering is less costly than traditional e-mail options because it does not provide any e-mail storage. And the employees don't have to maintain two e-mail boxes, yet can still send and receive Accenture-addressed e-mails.

Accenture conducts a complete review and update of all IT offerings in its catalog at least once a year. The review is led by the IT products and services steering committee, made up of IT professionals and chaired by the IT organization's executive director of business operations. The committee meets as needed during the year to hear presentations from product managers who are proposing new offerings or changes. Once the committee finalizes its menu of services and products, the IT Steering Committee then gives the final sign-off on the offerings.

IT standards and architecture

With input from the businesses and based on market developments, the IT organization sets IT standards for all technology components used to run Accenture's business. These components include portal architecture, application styles, user interface designs, usability standards, architecture services and physical infrastructure. In addition, it uses the Accenture-standard methodology and tools for technology development and delivery. The ITSC reviews and approves major decisions.

CHAPTER 5: ADAPTING ACCENTURE'S IT GOVERNANCE TO OTHER ORGANIZATIONS

An effective IT governance model can put an organization on the path to high performance. Accenture's research on high performance businesses has established a strong link between high performance in IT and overall business excellence. With IT so critical, chief executives increasingly include high performance IT among their strategic imperatives, according to the research.

In addition to its research, Accenture's own experience is a testament to the power of smart IT governance in driving high performance IT and corporate high performance. Its IT governance model is world-class, with major benefits falling directly to the bottom-line while building organizational capabilities that will allow the company to outperform its peers over the long- term.

Whether public or private, for-profit or not-for-profit, no organization can ignore demands to raise performance. The struggling economy alone necessitates new ways to drive efficiency and productivity. But even in good times, pressure comes from donors and shareholders, employees, industry influencers, and most assuredly, from competitors.

While Accenture's complex business structure creates specific requirements for its IT governance model, other organizations can adapt many of its best practices to fit their needs. Both for organizations building their first governance model and for those wanting to take IT governance to a new level of effectiveness, six key lessons stand out:

1. Construct IT governance to parallel corporate governance

Accenture's corporate governance supports its centralized structure of global business processes. So IT governance echoes the same structure, with centralized bodies representing its geographies, businesses, corporate functions and users.

An IT governance structure that aligns with the corporate structure helps ensure effective and efficient decision-making and assigns responsibility and accountability that aligns with the business.

2. Align IT with business priorities

The vast majority of business leaders understand just how critical technology is to virtually every aspect of their operations. But these leaders are just as critical to technology's success.

Business involvement in IT projects ensures business and IT priorities are in sync and that the business is as committed to the IT projects' success as the IT organization. To focus its IT initiatives squarely on the business, Accenture created the roles of business sponsor and stakeholder. Business sponsors leverage technology to advance their operations while stakeholders ensure that the people who will use the technology participate in its development.

3. Involve top management

Organizations make two common mistakes with IT governance: 1) they leave IT decisions largely, or even entirely, to the IT department; and/or 2) they involve middle managers from the business. Neither works well because IT executives and mid-level managers do not have the broad and deep business insight or power necessary to set priorities and ensure strategic decisions that best support organizational objectives.

IT governance succeeds when executives at the most senior levels participate. And conversations in the hallway or elevator are not enough. Rather, leadership involvement needs to be regular and structured, such as membership on an IT Steering Committee.

Such a forum brings together an organization's top leaders to debate and resolve priorities. These senior executives understand their own operating unit's needs as well as those of the firm overall. They also have the authority to make things happen.

The direct support, guidance and personal involvement of senior management across Accenture have been indispensable to the effectiveness of its IT governance, and by extension, its IT. As the executive sponsor of its IT governance model, Accenture's COO has made it clear through words and action that IT governance is a priority. Similarly, the COOs of every business and the leaders of every corporate function participate in the ITSC because it gives them the opportunity to make decisions that affect Accenture's overall business as well as their own areas.

4. Make business leaders responsible for their IT projects

Making business executives responsible and accountable for requesting technology to support their operations is a formula for success. With this approach, IT initiatives are not perceived as being thrust on the business by the IT organization, but rather, as an integral part of the business growth plan and capability-building.

Accenture's IT governance relies on business sponsors to make IT projects their own and holds them accountable for their projects' effectiveness. With this vested interest, the business sponsors help drive implementation and adoption and strive to ensure the technology delivers value.

5. Involve all key constituencies

An effective IT governance model builds in representation from all stakeholders. With its diverse global workforce and disparate businesses, Accenture created mechanisms to tap perspectives from across its geographies, operating units, corporate functions and users. Stakeholders play a vital role at all levels of governance, including serving on the IT Steering Committee and IT project steering committees.

6. Get started

No IT governance model needs to be perfect on day one. Rather than develop a comprehensive model that covers every contingency, it often is easier to start with a more limited approach that quickly demonstrates its value to the organization. Accenture began by focusing its IT governance on IT investment prioritization and decision making and then expanded from there.

Optimizing IT with smart governance

Technology is woven into the fabric of every enterprise these days, so IT decisions have far-reaching and long-lasting effects on an organization's competitiveness, bottom-line and ability to achieve strategic goals. IT governance is too important to leave uncoordinated and ad hoc.

Using Accenture as a model, organizations can make a compelling case for the need for IT governance and the elements of effective governance, including the involvement of senior corporate leaders. They can adapt Accenture's approach to develop IT governance that suits their needs, organizational structure and culture.

IT governance is a process, and it is vital to recognize that it will need to evolve along with the business and as the maturity of the IT function changes over time. Keeping IT governance in step with the business will keep it relevant, sustaining its ability to add business value. Taking this approach, an organization can help optimize the use and cost-effectiveness of technology to support key objectives and high performance.

ITG RESOURCES

IT Governance Ltd. sources, creates and delivers products and services to meet the real-world, evolving IT governance needs of today's organisations, directors, managers and practitioners.

The ITG website (*www.itgovernance.co.uk*) is the international one-stop-shop for corporate and IT governance information, advice, guidance, books, tools, training and consultancy.

www.itgovernance.co.uk/it_governance.aspx is the information page from our website for these resources.

Other Websites

Books and tools published by IT Governance Publishing (ITGP) are available from all business booksellers and are also immediately available from the following websites:

www.itgovernance.co.uk/catalog/355 provides information and online purchasing facilities for every currently available book published by ITGP.

www.itgovernanceusa.com is a US$-based website that delivers the full range of IT Governance products to North America, and ships from within the continental US.

www.itgovernanceasia.com provides a selected range of ITGP products specifically for customers in South Asia.

www.27001.com is the IT Governance Ltd. website that deals specifically with information security management, and ships from within the continental US.

Pocket Guides

For full details of the entire range of pocket guides, simply follow the links at *www.itgovernance.co.uk/publishing.aspx*.

Toolkits

ITG's unique range of toolkits includes the IT Governance Framework Toolkit, which contains all the tools and guidance that you will need in order to develop and implement an appropriate IT governance framework for your organisation. Full details can be found at *www.itgovernance.co.uk/products/519*.

For a free paper on how to use the proprietary Calder-Moir IT Governance Framework, and for a free trial version of the toolkit, see *www.itgovernance.co.uk/calder_moir.aspx*.

There is also a wide range of toolkits to simplify implementation of management systems, such as an ISO/IEC 27001 ISMS or a BS25999 BCMS, and these can all be viewed and purchased online at *www.itgovernance.co.uk/catalog/1*

Best Practice Reports

ITG's range of Best Practice Reports is now at *www.itgovernance.co.uk/best-practice- reports.aspx*. These offer you essential, pertinent, expertly researched information on an increasing number of key issues including Web 2.0 and Green IT.

Training and Consultancy

IT Governance also offers training and consultancy services across the entire spectrum of disciplines in the information governance arena. Details of training courses can be accessed at *www.itgovernance.co.uk/training.aspx*.

Descriptions of our consultancy services can be found at *www.itgovernance.co.uk/consulting.aspx*. Why not contact us to see how we could help you and your organisation?

Newsletter

IT governance is one of the hottest topics in business today, not least because it is also the fastest moving, so what better way to keep up than by subscribing to ITG's free monthly newsletter *Sentinel*? It provides monthly updates and resources across the whole spectrum of IT governance subject matter, including risk management, information security, ITIL and IT service management, project governance, compliance and so much more.

Subscribe for your free copy at
www.itgovernance.co.uk/newsletter.aspx.

EU for product safety is Stephen Evans, The Mill Enterprise Hub, Stagreenan, Drogheda, Co. Louth, A92 CD3D, Ireland. (servicecentre@itgovernance.eu)